WORMS, DIRT

Also by Daniel Barban Levin

Slonim Woods 9

WORMS, DIRT

DANIEL BARBAN LEVIN

Four Way Books
Tribeca

Library of Congress Cataloging-in-Publication Data

Names: Levin, Daniel Barban author
http://id.loc.gov/authorities/names/n2020060171
http://id.loc.gov/rwo/agents/n2020060171
Title: Worms, dirt / Daniel Barban Levin.
Description: New York : Four Way Books, 2026.
Identifiers: LCCN 2025027291 (print) | LCCN 2025027292 (ebook) | ISBN 9781961897748 trade paperback | ISBN 9781961897755 ebook
Subjects: LCGFT: Poetry
http://id.loc.gov/authorities/genreForms/gf2014026481
Classification: LCC PS3612.E92374 W67 2026 (print) | LCC PS3612.E92374 (ebook) | DDC 811/.6--dc23/eng/20250618
LC record available at https://lccn.loc.gov/2025027291
LC ebook record available at https://lccn.loc.gov/2025027292

This book is manufactured in the United States of America and printed on acid-free paper.

Four Way Books is a not-for-profit literary press. We are grateful for the assistance we receive from individual donors, public arts agencies, and private foundations including the New York State Council on the Arts, a state agency.

We are a proud member of the Community of Literary Magazines and Presses.

Contents

III

Maybe They Feel the Same Way

I only want the approval of the people who treated me worst

The person who broke my heart
The person who hurt my friends

If they read this and say

Wow

I will be fine
I will be alright forever

Instead, should I want to impress
The people I hurt

So I can feel I repaired
Any harm I caused?

Yes

But I never treated anyone badly
Or did anything wrong
In my entire life

I

The Leavings

"Currently, dung beetles are the only animals we know of that use the Milky Way for reliable orientation. They are excellent little astronomers."
—James Foster, University of Konstanz

When I started to write a book
          about the past few years,
I didn't know you.

          I didn't know it would end
With us two. I thought I would write

          about the cult I was in,
Then left,
          and the breakups:

Left on the airplane, left after signing the lease;
          leavings, leavings, it would be

About all of these, and I would
          call it that: *the leavings*. A joke.
An undercut. Then I found out

          Wendell Barry beat me to it.
"Even better," I thought. "More leavings."

Years ago, I got a Venmo from you,
The memo: “Worms, dirt.” What was it for?
I crane to recall as if

The past is behind a wall
which is slowly growing taller.

A road trip. We hiked Fern Canyon.
That’s it. We crossed the river again and again,
Walls quivering, a blind spectacle of

light and droplets. That is the quality
Of the memory, its texture.

We hiked until there were no more
Tourists, families, couples posing
with ancient driftwood, and it was silent

Except for our clothes rustling
and a low static we couldn’t identify.

We rounded a bend. We could go
no further because the cliff had sheared
Into the river.

What remained was an open-face dollhouse.
Centipedes and mealworms writhed

in rooms they'd carved exactly their size.
Cut crosswise,
the world reveals itself to be

Digestive, constantly undergoing revision.
Two years later, we live together.

Sometimes I'm convinced
I must have fallen, hit my head,
And I will wake up any minute.

Where is the end of loss? To leave, to be left,
You must arrive.

I thought love was self-sufficient,
It broke the laws
of conservation;

It self-fertilized
like certain species of jellyfish or the virgin

Mary. But of course, it doesn't.
            Love requires
What poems are made of,

            what you're looking at right now.
I'm a dung beetle,

            fighting off flies,
Rolling my precious,
            massive ball of shit

In the direction
            of the oldest light.

Candy

When I was a kid, I would hide in the bathroom and rail
little red boxes of Sun-Maid raisins. I would read the backs
Over and over like shampoo bottles. Sun-dried! Imagine:

thousands of grapes laid out withering into these deershit-
Adjacent gems. I pretended to find them on the ground like garnets

which, supposedly, in parts of Colorado, litter the surface
Of the earth. Raisins! Raisins everywhere! I cared not for the flesh
of the grape: too taut, too plump, too shot through with juice,

A child's fruit. Sometimes, though, I admit, I would sneak downstairs,
upturn the miniature box—practically a joke, the size of that box,

A snack for dolls—into a Styrofoam bowl, cover it with half an inch
of water, some brown sugar, and microwave it until the raisins
Revived, Frankensteinian, to a form of life not the same as before,

but more powerful, perverted. I sat in the bathroom
Every morning before school and shit my brains out until

my parents made me come downstairs. I didn't want to be sick,
I didn't think about it that hard. I would use my teeth to slit
the edge of a raisin, extrude its contents like glow from a bug

Or the last nurdle of toothpaste from the tube, then discard the hollow skin
 like the abandoned husks of cicadas I'd find all over the woods

Which resembled the real thing so precisely they might as well have been...
 The truth is I couldn't kill myself, so I wanted to be emptied as
Completely as the red boxes I'd produce every day. I counted, the most

 I ate in one sitting was 23. My mom kept buying and buying
And buying the bags they came in, at least three in our house

 at all times. Why? I remember her looking at the sugar content
Of each item in the grocery store, rejecting one thing after another that
 I wanted, I wanted, I wanted but already I was beginning to learn

How to narrow my desire. My mother's family heirloom.
 Legs dangling in the cart, cold metal on my thighs. There it was:

The talisman of my affection, the bastion of my grief, the red bag
 in supermarket light, the taste of cinnamon bread, sweetness, relief.
"These," she said, throwing three in the cart, "are nature's candy."

True Crime

You're national news. You're ignoring the voicemail
        from the FBI. The agent's name is Kelly Maguire.
She wants to talk about what happened to you.

        As you walk home with the roommate you barely talk to,
He says, "Your life is entering the zeitgeist now."

        He just wanted an excuse to say "zeitgeist," you're pretty sure.
You let yourself imagine, for only a moment, how many people
        are talking about you. How many of them work for the FBI?

You're like someone who fell into a well, got stuck
        for a year or two, climbed out, and didn't mention

Other people lived down there too. You thought that
        if you did, those people would kill you.
Orange peels on your bedside table. Empty cans.

        The curtain drawn 'til noon. Ignoring a voicemail
From the FBI. In LA, everyone looks straight out of central casting.

        You used to believe California was a dramatic place for
Dramatic people. The earthquakes and the fires made them
        lose perspective. Within six months of moving here,

You're living a procedural crime drama and ignoring an agent.
          How many people are talking to how many people about

How many people are talking about you right now?
          You went to a screening in the graveyard and realized
These are all just theater kids. A producer called Amazon Studios

          "brave." In the background, an actor was making ice cream
With liquid nitrogen. You're getting the sense everyone in this town

          wants to be talked about. A voicemail on their phone
From an agent. You used to wish to be happy
          then someone told you he knew how. You didn't notice

His voice was coming from a hole in the ground.
          You are picking up the phone now.

When I Left a Cult for the North Country

No one seemed surprised by the cluster flies.
Even while they whirred on the floor in loud, wide circles,
No one mentioned a thing.

Someone talked to me about wood, someone noticed
My winter coat. They called that "a good layer,"

they called it "gear," but nothing about the flies.
Never entirely alive, the flies outlined each room like molding.
No one sold fly swatters up there either, isn't that weird?

Not even Walmart. They expected you to sweep them
up still buzzing, I guess, let them go nuts inside

Your dirt devil. Are they in the drains? Maybe they
get in that way. Are they in my bed? My landlord
Put a windshield scraper in my letterbox—

real nice. My boss lent me snow shoes, a heat pad for
My feet—"thank you," I said. But I would not be keeping these

gifts long. The flies, like me, only arrived
After a wrong turn in a dark pipe,
trying to remember how to stay alive.

One Year in New Hampshire

Through my bathroom window, a snowcapped mountain like the glossed shoulder
Of a grand piano hunches behind the horizon. I go to therapy for the second time
And my therapist tells me her marriage isn't working. My ceilings lower.

In the back of my bedroom a buzzing turns up in volume until my neighbors scream
At someone through a car window and the car peels off. Red blinking on my wall.

A trailer emblazoned for Trump parked outside my house. The river is wide and cold
And drowned a horse once. It broke its leg and fell so its nostrils faced upstream.
This is a town in the north which draws tourists for winter. It's not winter now,

But it's always cold enough to snow without notice. Raspberry soft serve. Tiger lilies
And lupines. A bear that lopes across the dirt road I think at first is just another lost dog.

I watch a man sitting outside holding a hand mirror in one hand and
trimming his beard
With a pair of tiny scissors in the other. I realize for the first time that the
people who warn
Me about other people wanting to seduce me are the people who want to
seduce me.

A man invites me to dinner at his farmhouse and in his car, I stab the side
of his throat
With my mother's fabric scissors. These are not my fingernails. My boss
comes over

And traces the shape of my car on a piece of wood. She gives me an
ottoman I don't want
With a secret compartment inside, then invites me to her house and makes
me watch a show
Called *Naked and Afraid*. She has rigged a tinfoil satellite on her roof which
she points

To the coordinates of any major television studio. My girlfriend enters a
period of not
Sleeping with me which begins now and ends when I move away to
California.

I hike for hours and when I reach the waterfall, it's frozen. Standing on the river's
Choked-up throat, I take a short, grainy video. The day I move, my boss's dog dies,
And when I go outside, my car is encased in a pine tree. I've lived next to the only

Graveyard in town this whole time. My breath catches as I drive away. I held it often,
Not knowing why, as if I were underwater. My therapist says she hopes we can still be

Friends as she begins to pull her skirt up. When I shut my eyes and she puts her tongue
On my tongue, I'm inside the mountain, staring out through miles of nothing.
The rocks here are so dark they look wet. Put them in your mouth and they change

Color, revealing a picture you haven't seen yet. I woke up one morning
Years after having left and found two of those stones drying on my doorstep.

Camel Drawing

First, I have to remember what a camel looks like.
It's already outlandish enough that they have one hump,
I can't believe I'm giving this camel two. Do you sit in between

the humps or on top of them? Some things seem so obvious,
You don't notice when they stop being obvious at all.

We don't know whether dinosaurs had humps because fat doesn't
Fossilize. In the future, when the camel's visage is long forgotten,
scientists will draw it like a busted horse. Not me, I'm giving this thing

Three humps, why not? I'm lying across all three of them.
The camel doesn't like it. His tongue is sticking out. Lolling, even.

I should give this camel a little personality. Here: his vibe is
determined, a little aloof. He's a real survivor. He's like,
"Oh, water? I could have some, but I just had a drink

a month ago." This camel won't win any beauty pageants,
But he will tell you that camel beauty pageants are a degrading practice—

he can feel beautiful without any patterns shorn into his fur.
Sorry, I don't mean to demean a practice I know nothing about.

I gesture with my pencil, "Come back here, camel.

That's alright. Sit there." Now, he's sitting like a human. He's come to like
his new apartment, his new neighborhood. He doesn't quite

Fit into most of the furniture, but that's okay. That's fine. His toes
have a hard time finding purchase on the wood floors.
He's been picking up new hobbies. He's trying

to model his life after the alpaca he met once
On a trip to Peru. He's heard that at the mall

nearby they shoot real snow at you, and he thinks
About going there. He misses the cold desert nights,
sitting on his tail, huddled close to other camels like a

Bunch of penguins. He misses other camels, basically.
His forehead has started to feel a little hard and

One morning, he touches his temples to find fat pencils growing there.
"It's finally happening," he thinks. "I'm turning into a giraffe."
He'll have to move into an apartment with higher ceilings.

He'll have to slam his neck into another male's neck
For dominance. He rubs his neck. He doesn't want to slam it

into anything. He isn't interested in seeing the tops of trees
Or the bald spots on people's heads. He facetimes his mom
who, recently, in a video she sent him, pretended to be a lion.

She never has before, but this, he hopes, *this* she might understand.
She doesn't recognize him in the facetime, so he calls her back

On the phone. "Who was your friend?" she asks. He tries to bury his face
in his hands, but he's afraid to touch the tender, aching stalks.
Stretch marks have been appearing on his neck. He goes to the shed,

gets the saw, sits in front of the mirror. "First, I have to remember
What a camel looks like," he says, then begins to draw.

Portrait of the Author as a Young Man Contractually Bound to Write a Memoir

Here is the print I leave in the sand, cold and wet. Here is my chest and here, the wind
        palpitating against my chest. Up on the tsunami line, Faith mounts her installation,
The most recent in a series about nostalgia. Photographs of [this beach] [her face] [a room

        she had to sneak into] all hang about a small, gauzy tent, frames clanking, threads
Tangled by a seaward wind. The sirens begin to wail their round wails which return to the

        point where they began and then begin again. The feeling I'm trying to describe is
The feeling of advancing into the thing that's bound to kill you, ignoring calls to turn around.
        At a certain point you can plumb the past so deep you begin to drown.

Still Life

after Brecht's "Five Difficulties in Writing the Truth"

There's nothing wrong with painting a still life
        on a sinking ship as long as someone else is
Bailing out water, someone's screaming for help,

        someone's shooting a flare to light the moonless
Night. This is what I tell myself. If you're alone on the ship and

        you *want* to die, painting is, in fact, a positive sign.
Let's say there's shore, a crowd gathering. At the welcome home party,
        everyone shouts, "Speech! Speech!" They clang so rambunctiously

With their knives, broken glass flies everywhere. Drenched in champagne
        and paint, you launch dutifully into the speech Antony makes

Over Caesar's body in which he explains that both his heart
        and Caesar's good deeds will be buried with Caesar's bones.
But that's not right. You switch to Artabanus's speech about Persia

        in which he says the greater a tree or a house,
The more likely it is to be struck by lightning, but wait,
        no, not that one. Is it Pyrrhus's speech? No. Must be Hamlet?

The reality is you're sitting on a couch with a cat under your legs,
          unable to move, less and less interested in cunning, the acrobatics

Required to make a meal out of the truth. You're alone.
          Look at it. Just eat it. It's fine. It's simple. It's three layers
Of some kind of corn cake with green leaves in between.

Hell

"No one knows a tarantula's lifespan in the wild,
        they outlive the scientists who tag and track them."
Roger, my new roommate, lifts a textbook off the tank.

        Inside is what looks like a shriveled gorilla's paw.
I'm subletting Roger's second bedroom after the breakup

        and I'm realizing I know absolutely nothing about him.
While I'm standing with Roger and his spider in Los Angeles,
        I'm also in Texas, and it's a hot day a couple months back;

I'm watching her sweep up spiders in a short dress.
        I had been trying to read but couldn't stop looking

At her. At them. At her. "I'm killing them now,
        there are just too many," she said.
"...Spiders store memories in their webs,"

        Roger says which, again, seems unlikely.
"Some drink nectar from flowers."

        He affectionately touches the hairs
On the spider's back, which move.
        "Not her, though."

The man from the taco truck
        ran to our car, hands above his head,

A mango in each, yelling, “Muchos mangos!”
        We ate them over her sink, copper
Streaming down our necks. They were free and we were

        broke. It was like eating our hearts: soft, noisy, gross.
Roger replaces the tarantula gently in her cell.

        She touches a branch, the glass, gingerly as if blind.
She can touch eight different things at the same time.
        “They feel no pain,” he says. “Without pain, they have no memory.

No need. Unless you consider memory to be
        knowing where you stowed your lunch.”

He replaces the book, the ceiling of her cell,
        then looks at me, seeing something I have yet to see myself.
“Living like that,” he says, “must be hell.”

Memoir

I opened the door and watched myself
taking a bath. "I look sad," I said. Nothing had
Happened, not yet. I saw through

my past. The book I was bound to write,
I'd already written it. I shook it above my head.

The answers fluttered out
Like every apology
no one's ever received.

I'm on the approach, a camera
imitating vertigo, pulling away

While zooming in close. A something white, uncertain,
melting from the surface like foam or snow.
The room overflows with déjà vu.

I wanted to erase someone from my memory.
I can't for the life of me remember who.

II

Quicksand Fetish

I wake up still thinking about the quicksand fetish community.
According to the forums, there are "sinkers" and there are "watchers."
She's sleeping, face turned toward the cinder block wall.

Everything can be categorized. I sleep on the outside, for example,
because I always wake before her, and then I don't know what to do

Except kind of stare into space. I make her coffee, toss the grounds
into the flowerpot. Sinkers have an online catalogue documenting
All the best spots, how deep they are, how far from the road,

where to park for free, how to breathe, everything you need
To drown in the ground in a way that's safe, economical, and technically

legal. The watchers use it too, but that's frowned upon. Sinkers aren't
Sinking for anyone but themselves. We were in school, living far apart.
I came to Texas for her birthday, and she seemed almost surprised to

See me. She keeps blinking as if there's a bright light positioned
right behind me. Sinkers describe a "moment of acceptance," or,

"Total surrender." Your eyes close, the earth rises around you,
and you have this vision in which you emerge on the other side
In another life, the life you were meant to live, the alternate path

you could have taken when the road forked
But you didn't, you took this one.

She's been apologizing to me continuously
For no reason, as far as I can tell. She keeps getting motion sick
standing still. I get up quietly, go to the bathroom, sit.

What the watcher is after is this: through the jungle he hears a struggle
and rushes toward it, batting leaves out of his face. When he arrives,

The last bubbles are breaking on the surface of the mud. He plunges
a hand in deep, all the way down to the shoulder, touching...what?
The watcher wants someone right in front of him and just out of reach.

He wants to lie cheek to the dirt, full of regret for years.
Trust me. I'm face-to-face with her mirror, an oval pool of shining mud.

I thought the next step was simple. One of us would have to leave;
One would have to watch. But I was wrong. There were three of us
all along. I can hear him now, coming through the trees.

The Beginning of the End

I know it wasn't when I lost her house keys
After we'd been making out on the golf course.
Or when we snuck back over the fence.

When we sat on her stoop underneath the tree
That had split down the middle but still stood,

two halves leaning dangerously away from one another,
It wasn't then. Occasionally, they sprouted
small, sad branches that looked like weeds.

Not while we waited in the waning heat.
Not when I skipped class to take her to the ocean.

I carried her into the water, our clothes draped in a cave.
Her dad's fear of sharks was so intense that the only time she'd seen him in the ocean
Was when he taught her and her sister to swim. "This is as far as I'll go,"

He'd said, holding them in the waves, eyes darting around.
Not at the party in Austin when Luke lined up the coke.

Not afterwards, at home, when they kissed, then fucked,
Their breathing congested, strange.

Earlier than that, at least.

Not when we all half-slept in her bed, a kung fu movie on the TV.
When Tony Jaa kicked someone into a wall of lightbulbs, Luke said,

"that's what I feel like should be
done to me."
Apropos of nothing, he said it. I handed him my diary and a saw.

"This will make you feel better,"
I said.

Not then, but close.
I laid in her bed facing away, wondering what to call this
feeling. Like I'd gotten off a plane in the wrong city.

No one would look me in the face. Nothing made sense. The water bug
crawling up her
cinderblock wall was improbably large. Texas.

What a shithole in the summer—just a series of incandescent, sweaty
rooms and bars
seething. The water bug was too big. It shouldn't have been able to fly.
"It shouldn't be able to fly," I thought, even as I watched its wings unfurl.

Two months earlier, she had rented a bounce house for a friend's birthday.
As we lay in the pink light of that soft, translucent castle,

Neither of us said anything. I couldn't think of anything worth saying.
I was lying in a bounce house, and I felt like a pest.
So, that was it. It must have been then.

Turtle

When I tried to escape it was always this
        or that. The urge to leave was an alarm
I thought was broken, signaling nothing.

        I'd be holding a coffee in one hand,
In the other balancing a pile of books

        when it would chime once, quietly,
"Maybe I imagined..." then a few seconds later,
        it chimed again. I didn't say anything

To anyone. It occurred to me, but I was afraid to try.
        Everything I touched screamed.

After I left, other sounds came through: forks clinking
        against porcelain bowls, a loaf of bread ripped in two,
The murmur of people talking in the morning.

        I wanted to eat it all up; I wanted to slurp the scenery
Like a bowl of soup. But I was afraid—

        afraid to try, afraid to move, afraid if I turned to look,
I might see the truth: that I had never actually left,
        nothing had changed. What if no one had trapped me,

Not really? It kept happening again and again,
so I must be doing it to myself.

Why couldn't I tell the difference between the trap
and everything else? Like those desperate
Turtles at the impossible market downtown,

I was born inside it,
Only capable of growing as large as my enclosure.

I chewed lettuce. I felt in my spine
That things could somehow
be better. I heard something

Ringing. I was finally free, I thought.
I didn't realize I'd been bought.

What Remains

I got myself lost in the woods
          over and over again—
turned this way

          and that. There was no path,
Only mishappen trees

          bent to the outline of
My mother's totaled car.
          Why did she crash?

She lost control of the car
          about half the time

She drove me home from school—
          it's not easy
To explain anything

          you can't get outside of.
I became observant,

          found impressions in the grass
Where origami deer crooked
          sleeping limbs beneath

Soft, dew-wet tummies, their beds
        beside the logs the fire department left

The night they felled the tree
        that was engulfed from within.
From the outside, it looked fine,

        but I saw the hole in its heart
glow with its own light.

        I wanted them to let it burn.
I wanted to crawl inside.
        The only thing I understood,

As with so many times in my life,
        was mom was still alive.

Life goes on. The forest changes.
        The trees are overtaken by vines
Of poison ivy like hairy veins, the underside

        of a cock. Stuck in the mud,
I found a turtle shell, bleached, spine intact.

I perched on the stump a long time
Thinking about touching it.
I feared neither curses nor germs;

I feared the sound I'd heard that night
of a girl or a fox screaming

And the silence after
Mom's car hit the tree.
Weird, a kind of murmur, the memory:

somebody's parents asking their child to lie
To authorities. "An animal darted in front of the car,

Mom swerved to avoid it."
I betrayed the things that lived how I wished I could.
In the woods. In spite of us. They haunted me.

Take the turtle shell home and some soft,
spineless, naked thing would follow me,
Rack its soft head against the window,

begging for its back.
I began to insist I could be a bear.

"I could be a bear," I'd say, out loud to no one.
I could eat berries. I could hunt fish in the crick.
I could sleep through what I couldn't survive.

I pressed on her legs, trying to work the gas and brake,
but she was Mom. She wanted to drive.

I stepped out of the car into the street
strewn with glass, shreds of hide, puffs of fur
Like snow, sugar syrup, like ornaments and tinsel draped upon

the tree. It began to smoke.
I was not a child anymore, not a bear either.

What was taken from me?
I still don't know.
We got lost in the woods on the way home.

There was no path. She drove.
Things darted through the smoke. I ran between

The car and the trees, reaching up
to tap on the window. I let her know
She's close to the edge of the road.

Haunting

A ghost lives in my body
          where I thought I lived.
It's easy to forget that

          when I feel nothing, I'm
Not doing very well, mouthing my

          own name from below a cascade
Of information: news and TV
          and jokes and TV and news

And news and falling asleep
          to the sound of people

I don't know chatting
          about topics that affect me
Only indirectly. The ghost

          in my body wants me to move on,
Wants me to stay the same,

          has almost given up on me,
Finally. The ghost takes me out
          on the town. "Hello, lovely,

What an evening," the ghost
makes me say, but my jaw

Wags at no one, the bar deserted.
The ghost has trouble lining up
Its eyes up with my eyes.

"I've got no one but you, Ghost,"
I say, attempting to cradle it with my

Whole body. In spite of everything,
I begin to remember. I can feel the ghost
straining like a mussel

Pulled by the tide—all it is

is holding on. The ghost gets thinner and thinner

And when I can hardly feel it anymore,
the past steps through it
as through a pair of gauzy curtains onto a stage.

The past is clearly accustomed
To making two things:

dramatic entrances and everything
About itself.
As it begins its monologue, it gesticulates

Grotesquely. I can't describe what that looks like.
"In Hell," says the past, "time is an iceberg

"On a great, opaque sea." The past is holding a series of masks
which it changes with great ceremony.
"In Heaven,

time is a joke the angels tell." It looks around
As if expecting a laugh.

Disappointed, it moves on.
From the audience, I cough.
The past whips around. It seems annoyed,

But what appeared unrelenting
gives way to weariness.

The past predicts my first question. "The ghost
was only doing its job," says the past.
"What was that?" I ask.

The past looks guilty. I wonder if
The ghost will ever come back.

I can't believe I miss it. "What was
its job?" I ask, looking hard at the past.
"To protect you," the past explains,

beginning to pull the curtains back,
"from me."

The Man

You have to reconstruct the man. You have to put him back together piece by
Piece even though you spent each day since it happened deconstructing him.
After so many years pretending he didn't exist, you observe him up close.

Something's wrong. He's too small. You check the instructions, the list of
Parts. Did you drop something? You look around, press your cheek against

The floor. No. So, he was always this size. When a man makes you afraid
Of his body, it expands in your memory. In turn, your body deflates
Until it's small enough to vanish completely. Your body was 19 years old.

Your body was like a grave marker for a childhood that was about to be
Interred. He placed his hand on your face. You shuddered. The hands

Of a man, the face of a child. The hands were enormous, you thought.
The fingers were blunt. Was any of it right? Did any of it happen the way
You remembered? The piece you still can't find. It must be true. He was

Gentle. Sometimes, he was gentle. You can't find it. The hands' capacity
For gentleness even as you watched them, in disbelief, dismantle you.

Making Dinner, I Thought I Had Loved

        but I hadn't. I thought (even more deleteriously)
That I'd been loved but of course,
        I hadn't. I raked my fingers through

The spaghetti to comb it straight, each strand
        my life and what it could be, so fragile, so *al dente*

Which is to say, *of the teeth*, so when I toss it all
        at the wall, it's as likely to stick as to fall.
I believed life was one thing and then, like nothing,

        it wasn't. It's something, now. Isn't it something?
To be alive, to live twice, inside and outside the shells

        of your own belief. I can't believe it!
I want to know what love is. I know you can't
        show me. But lord, do I wish someone could.

Addiction

Inhale and I'm back at the riverbank
where I grew up, scrambling the cliff

Calf-deep in terra-cotta
water, sculpting hard,
Slick muck from underneath the bridge.

The river between the house and the road
Ran through clay, swamp grass, and skunk cabbage.

I never saw where it ends.
It's still hard to imagine, a foot or two wide,
joining other streams, gathering force, concussive

Falls, clouds of steam, taste of salt. I just stood at the head
and bent a fishhook from a paperclip

which trailed from a long, thin, invisible thread.
I held it in the water, wanting so badly to feel something
It was almost like feeling something.

A Brief Stint of Stealing

So quickly something transforms
From unimaginable to normal.
One day, it makes you sweat

Like a cold plum to think
you accidentally stole a hat

From the store by walking out
with it on your head. A few weeks later,
Most of your take-home from work

you've skimmed like froth off a pool
That's undergone a sudden shift

from basic to acidic.
Either, you have learned,
being extremes, burn.

Back East for the Wedding, I Visit My Parents

Look: a window from the treehouse we never built shattered in the grass.
Patches of sky tangled in years of overgrowth. All I think about is a past

That shouldn't have happened, which is so far removed from the past that
Should have happened, it's been easy to keep hidden. No one assumes the
Absolute worst; they haven't enough creativity. The treehouse: one board

Between two trees that over the years drifted downhill at different speeds.
Stupid college kids, dreamy and soft focus, falling in love and losing virginities,

Screaming and doing drugs and hugging drunk. A world temporarily without
Consequences. A pane of glass held up against the sky, visible when its edges
Catch the light. Here are the notes for the book I am supposed to write:

How It Feels

Like letting all your plants die when it's raining outside.
Like tearing out the voice box of a songbird—no, all the songbirds—

    and playing opera over giant loudspeakers.
Like blowing dozens of intricate glass unicorns
    so you can throw them at a charging bull.

Like blowing a real unicorn.
Like getting a word into the dictionary

    right before the collapse of civilization.
Like smiling so wide all your teeth fall out.
Like your teeth arranging themselves on the floor

    into the sentence you have never been able to say or write.
Like your brain just not working that way. Like finding a hallway

    in the back of your closet that leads to an empty observation room.
    Three swivel chairs behind a desk, one still spinning,
    a cup of coffee steaming next to the controls.

    You sit, take a sip, and begin your shift.
Like you were going to turn into a prince or a princess

or a pumpkin or a carriage or an ogre or a mermaid or a frog
or a human being but instead you never left the house.
You fell asleep at 10:30 and stayed exactly what you are.

Like you're having the best sex of your life
and suddenly there's a whole country in the way.

Like your parents incrementally cut off pieces
of your blanket until you forget it exists.
The things you love grow

smaller until they disappear.
Like snow.

Like burying your history in the yard
then years later adopting a dog to find it.
Like only crying when it's funny.

Like seeing the light at the end of the tunnel and realizing it's a fire.
Everything still happens despite your best efforts to stop it.

Like walking a mile to find the nearest farmhouse.
Like lowering the bucket into the well
when your hand slips and the rope unspools in a blur.

Like your whole town gathering in the street to sing rounds
    of *Row, Row, Row Your Boat* until you run off screaming.

Like the moment just before things get much, much worse—
    just before you panic and right after you understand fully.
Like watching a circus elephant lose its balance.

Like setting up your tent alone in the desert,
    and as you settle down for the night,

    you see a thunderstorm in the distance,
    and think about the cracked earth,
    and that sign you passed a few miles back.

Like the months you spent building a catapult for this siege
    with your medieval buddies and when it's ready,

    they face it towards the castle wall,
    draw down the arm with its little basket,
    and they all turn to you and say, "Get in."

Like you contract flesh-eating bacteria
    and after it completely consumes you,

the person you've always loved
falls in love with the bacteria.
Like smoking your own ashes.

Like building an airplane as you fly it except
you're no pilot so you call into the cabin,

"Does anybody know how to fly a plane?"
and there's nobody back there.
Like a ghost who never had a body trying to fit in.

Like your cousin has been keeping an exhaustive family tree
and you're not on it.

Like everyone is telling embarrassing stories
and you just can't think of one.
Like every story is embarrassing.

Like every morning, your roommate comes out of their room,
flips a switch on the wall,

and nothing happens.
One day you flip the switch
and nothing happens.

Like sending letters
to your postal worker.

Like that candle you never light.
Like thinking you grew up too fast,
then realizing you never grew up at all.

Like spelling your own name wrong.
Like opening a box

that's always been closed
and inside,
there's another box.

Like noticing yourself using the same words
over and over,

but you just can't stop.
Like mowing the lawn
with tweezers.

Like you pass out all the time
but if you take the pill in your hand,
you'll never sleep again.

Like your only skill is carving wood
back into the shape of a tree.
Like even if you try something different,

it's a tree. It's always a tree.
Like someone starts to interrupt

what you're doing
so you hold up a finger
silencing them,

even though you weren't doing anything.
Like after living in this lonely town for years,

you discover a long, twisting road ending in a set of stairs
behind a series of bungalows. You pass through
what seem to be private gates,

but they're adorned with reassuring signs,
and you arrive at a park you've never seen.

Like someone who you once loved
glimpsed through a crowd in a foreign city.

Like someone who wanders in from the street,
        claps their hands, and yells, “Show’s over, folks!”
        and it isn’t.

First Draft

Let's build the apartment where it happened. Let's start there and not even say
What went down in any amount of detail. Rooms are innocuous. Space doesn't
Have meaning until we ascribe meaning to it. Okay. I am sitting on the couch,

There. It's a black leather couch. It's soft and a little worn. Do you feel it?
Where did I enter? Through the only door in or out. There's plastic between

The frame and the door. Some kind of construction must be going on inside.
Don't forget, to enter the lobby, you have to exit New York City. It's New York
Outside. Look through the plate glass windows. The buildings in fog are masts

Of ships about to sink. Birds wheel the way they have always done. In spite of
Everything that indicates the contrary, this is not where you are going to die.

III

On The Roof

In Los Angeles, some people whisper soothing things
to their tap water. They call it by sweet names. They remind it
of mountain springs and thunderous waterfalls.

"That makes it taste better," Roger told me.
"And maybe some kind of health benefits."

I was watching cops break up an encampment,
They were throwing people's worldly belongings
Into a dumpster marked "Party Supplies."

This is the delusion behind my writing:
What I name the world might change it.

The Room Is Full

Beyond it is another room,
Also full. Beyond it is another
Room, also full. Beyond it is
Another room, also full, and beyond it

Is another room, also full, and beyond
It is another room, also full and
Beyond it is another room, also full, and
Beyond it is another room, also full,
And beyond it is another room,
Also full. Beyond it is another
Room, also full, and beyond it is
Another room, also full, and beyond it

Is another room, also full, and beyond
It is only this.

The Room

Like anything, it needs a recognizable shape, a region
We can navigate eyes closed and know what we're bumping
Into. The page is rectangular, sure, like the room, but the

Page doesn't contain the shelf, nor the bottle
Of pill capsules on the shelf. Until now.

A metaphor corners a subject by straying away from it,
The subject in this case being my own memories. The
drugs, the page, none of it is here. That was years ago.

There was a room. I lived there.
Now, I can't find it anymore.

Whale

I've watched the current gather like an invisible wing.
I've known whole novels told in light and darkness
And the movement through water of ink.

I don't need a story to tell—it's being told
Around me constantly. Krill in the millions

Survive in my mouth. While I sleep, the ocean
Turns to vapor then condenses to liquid again.
I have a destination and it is deep, deep, deep

Down below. It involves my flesh turning to snow,
Feeding my friends for six months or so.

An entire season made from my body.
It's gruesome until it empties of gruesomeness.
In this it is like living. The pressure is a mouth

Clamped shut around each word I'm about
To say right before it can be pronounced.

Looking Out My Window at Night in Los Angeles

I get immense relief from the matrix of lights
Formed by Glendale Boulevard: trapezoid of red
Stoplights and brake lights through the mountains

—fractures of light—lightning returning from the ground.
The headlamps: white, cream, some linen, lavender,

Robin's egg, pairs of them like siblings, and motorcycles
(Only children) widening as they approach then going
Cross-eyed. They pass beside the McDonald's sign.

They pass like a brief summer breeze the cold hollows
Of cars parked forever. And then they're gone, vanished

Beneath the bridge my window overlooks. Two times,
I've seen someone standing there, looking where I look,
And I've had to run outside to stop them from jumping.

One Day in New York

Going into the courthouse,
Sheets of snow
Fall from the roof

Twenty-seven floors above
With loud THWUMPS.

"Lawyer or witness?"
The security guard asks.
"Witness," I say.

He waves me through the gate.
THWUMP

As I collect my belongings
From the little basket, he asks
The other security guard,

"Hey, you ever seen a jumper?"
"No," the other guard says,

"But I've seen after."
The first guard is glad.
"I have," he says, THWUMP

then he gestures outside.
"It sounds just like that."

Peruvian Pepper Tree

This tree is packed with birds, mostly doves,
Eating the little pink kernels.
Their beaks can't taste the molecule

Which makes pepper burn.
Then they all fly away at once, which is good.

They'll bring the seeds somewhere else.
This tree was imported but isn't invasive.
A crucial difference to someone like me.

It's weird that we don't talk about how
Many pretty things are spread by shit.

Della SheriLove Creech (Rejoice in the Lamb)

after Christopher Smart

For I will consider my cat Della SheriLove Creech

For she is the first cat I've had since Pilot and Jammer who, despite
sounding like, ironically and confusingly, World War 1
dogfighters, were named by my older brother after the Stone
Temple Pilots and Pearl Jam

For last night, my brother on the phone said, "That's Dan's move, he takes
them on a road trip then he moves in with them"

For I have had many heartbreaks and until now, have never moved in with
anyone

For over fried chicken, before we picked up Della from the foster, Mary
asked if I held onto it, when my brother said that kind of thing,
and I said sometimes when you think you're not blaming anyone
you're blaming yourself

For Della turns out to be the color of the clouds we saw driving to Marina
Del Rey, dark and mottled against the afterglow

For she did not pee on the ride home as we feared but instead pressed her body against mine and sniffed me through the carrier, and alternated popping her head out of the top and retreating

For she has a soul, Mary said

For Pilot and Jammer lived 15 years and would have lived longer had my mom not used them as scions of her eating disorder

For my brother is now fixated on limiting dopamine and "getting shredded"

For Della did not hide under the bed as I feared but instead inspected everything and would occasionally approach, lick, then run away

For I blamed myself, I told Mary, for not fitting in to my family, for never feeling comfortable, for I would hear my brother say something like that, something deeply insulting, and only register a sick feeling in my stomach, and wonder what was wrong with me

For I spent much of my adolescence in the bathroom sick or pretending to be

For Jammer, the orange one, would sometimes emerge from the woods while I was sitting against a tree and seem surprised, as if I had interceded upon his world, but he would accept me anyway, and sit with me while I tried to understand why I didn't want to go home

For when I imagined running away, I imagined taking them with me

For my mom would scream at them for eating food she had given

For Della, the cat, is trepidatious when it comes to the daybed, though she hopped on it once, and is more a fan of the chair

For she did run outside one time, this morning, as we left for work, but I suspect she did not know what she was doing

For she relished the opportunity to meet our neighbor

For she has moments when the soul goes out of her, and she is an animal

For she defends herself as if from nothing, but has yet to draw blood

For we have only had Della one day, the first of an unknowable number

For beginnings and endings are reminders of how little we can control

For a pet becomes the precious container for one's deepest needs, and love and security are not the worst things to need

For while researching Christopher Smart's "Jubilate Agno," famous for
his writing about his cat in the mid-1700's while confined for
insanity, I learned of his use of puns for the purpose of, said he,
"participating with the divine that exists within language," and
also for, "iterating both present and future simultaneously, that is,
to redeem time"

For he refers to the Magnificat, known as Mary's song, which is structured
as a Jewish hymn to be sung in the darkness of the morning

For I am trying to do nothing if not redeem time and participate with the
divine that exists within language

For I must be locked up, then

For Mary said she wants to be her best self for Della, having updated her
address with the post office

For I said a rising tide lifts all boats and Della is the moon

For we woke this morning at 5:30 a.m., and she licked my hand, then ran away

For she is the moon, she said

For I am at work, writing this

For I have accrued so many reasons to live

I'm Always Scaring My Landlord

This morning, I was sitting on the mud hill with the lupines
Reading in my slippers when Phoebe (that's my landlord), ducked
Under the bottlebrush to futz with some of the trash in the yard.

I have to watch my landlord silently, be careful not to spook her.
Phoebe has these pale eyes that don't seem to see anything

Until I'm right in front of her, then she gets scared, grabs her heart.
It makes me feel like I'm doing something wrong
Being on her property, which is how I feel with all landlords.

Still on the mud hill, I noticed a bunch of flapping and chirping next to me.
Trapped in the old, discarded chicken coop was a baby chickadee.

I opened the doors; I lifted the whole thing up.
The bird didn't seem able to figure out the chicken wire.
Its parents were on the other side, I realized,

Slamming against this boundary they couldn't comprehend,
Through which they could see and touch each other

But could never, as they understood it, be together again.
I managed to corner the chick. How awful it is
To have to produce terror, to swallow that

To save a life you have to scare something
Half to death. I got it in my hands. I tried to hold it

Tight the way I've seen people swaddle babies
Or hold chickens, their wings pinned down,
Which makes them calm and prevents them from

Injuring themselves. The chick was not calm.
Everything in it screamed I am about to die.

Its parents were hopping around me, testing,
Truly, whether they could kill me. I put the chick
On the roof of the coop. Then it was gone.

What I'm not saying is that this is the first day
In a long time I've gone outside before the sun

Was just about to set. My landlord's name
Is the name of a bird. It's morning and I'm on the hill
With the lupines, watching a phoebe sing, full grown.

If I hadn't been there, would the chick have died,
Its parents on the other side of some chicken wire?

“I wish I had parents like that,” I thought,
Then realized I do. Dumb and helpless
With their love.

Notes from the Tower of Babel

I've unearthed this after losing it and finding it
And losing it again. Moving makes familiar things
Look unfamiliar and things you thought were
Familiar look even more familiar than they looked
Before, set against a background which, though it
Resembles where you've lived less, resembles
Where you'd always imagined living more. So, things
Look more familiar in the sense that they look more
Like your dreams and less like your life, as you've known it.

Notes from the Tower of Babel

When the world ends, it sounds like a leaf blower starting up
Then never stopping. Even now, it still sounds like that.
You get used to it. The Sun used to rage millions of decibels
Which to us sounded like nothing, birds chirping, plants growing,
A couple on the sidewalk arguing about the music festival
Their neighbor wants to host and where they're going to put
The porta johns. These are the things I miss most. In the apocalypse,
What sucks isn't the broiling heat followed by ice age—
Not the summer when the snow piled so deep we could walk
To the observation deck of the Eiffel Tower, not the politicians
Jawing in front of a vinyl decal of a White House peeled open
Like a blooming onion, tower of flame shooting from the top.
We knew how to love, then. All the religions were right, every one,
And therefore all wrong in different ways. Remember when
All those people vanished into the sky? Look around. The snakes
And kingfishers and blowflies have the souls of our uncles and aunts—
You can see it in their beady, astonished eyes. The ones left over
Didn't really believe anything. I scratched all day and night on the wall
Like a deprived cat, doing something for years I might call prayer.
I didn't care about the spiral ears of god, my words catching there
Like burrs in the fur of a lamb. I wish I could say it was even about
Devotion to process. I just wanted to be loved. At the end, the true end,
As the pretentious scholars of the new ivory towers walk the long halls
In their flip-flops, stopping in the library lined with our vitrified brains,

Discussing the days which predated this new present, they will talk about Chartreuse. They will talk about the monks who, in the last hour, withdrew. You can still see their abbey, at the other end of this long, enclosed tube.

Stay

"I'd hate it if you said *leave it* to me
the way you'd say it to a dog," you said.

I thought for a second. "You'd hate it
if I said anything to you that way," I said.
You hadn't decided yet what word to use

For how your ex-husband treated you.
We all live with a collar around our necks,

A snapped leash. The dog in me knows how
To leave it. After so many attempts at naming
The world, that's the trick he's learned.

Turn at the end of the trail. Don't add
Or do anything more. I didn't know

I was waiting to hear the opposite
Said in just the right way. And you do,
You say it.

The Silk Floss Tree

By what should we measure a life? You know
What. Mary and I walked to the store this morning
For relief, but they had no cinnamon twists, and so
We left. We are not in the mood for anything less

Than exactly what we need. On the way out, a
Woman walked towards me, her neck craning
As she walked, she was looking back at a pair of dogs,
Which were cute, and when she was about to run

Into me, "excuse me," I said, in my sweetest voice.
"Sorry," she said. Automatically, I suppose, because
A second later, once she'd passed me, she turned again
With the stare of someone looking at something red

Hot, something that hurts to look at, something
Like a blade or a coal, something dangerous.
"Forgive me," she said, loudly. Sarcastically. I promise,
No one has ever made forgiveness sound so hateful.

When we got home, I said to Mary, "I know it is misplaced,
But I hate that woman. I hate her. She killed our cat," I said,
Joking, a little. Cresting the steps to our house, we passed
The silk floss tree. The silk floss tree's bark is green and

Warted with thorns. "Tree of Refuge" or "Sheltering Tree,"
Family to the baobab, the silk floss swells after rain, pregnant.
You could slice it, if you liked, being careful of the thorns,
Which are in some cases an inch long, and water would gush forth.

The tree's progeny and its sustenance is water. We protect things
Which sustain us. We are sustained by the things we protect.
In the backyard, I watch the pin cherries spread, a new sapling
Each season. They grow in a line, headed somewhere, in the direction

Of the light, I guess. More fertile soil. They know something
I don't. I kill one of them. It is in the way. I want to put my table there.
I want to host friends. The pin cherries produce nothing anyway except
More pin cherries. But I don't touch the last descendent in the line.

And I ask myself, what is a life measured by? The life it produces?
The silk floss tree produces pods which look like avocados, except
Inside these pods, rather than a fatty, green, edible substance, is the
So-called floss, a cottony fluff. It looks like cat fur. It grows, if you can

Imagine, on the cob. Kernels of tightly bound potential which, when
Disturbed, expand, catch the wind, gather in clumps and clouds in every
Corner of our yard and the stairs to the street, so when I come home,
I see them and I think, for a moment, they are Della, our cat, who

Died this week. I killed her, I had to kill her, we killed her, our dog
Killed her, our dog caught her in its jaws and, our dog, our sweet pink-
Bellied pit bull, our idiot, who snorts and lows like a cow in spring,
Our dog of the iron jaw, who cannot help it, who was overcoming

A received reputation, who is kind to everyone except the cat
Who leapt over the gate while I was in the bathroom, who wanted to
See me, one last time, though she did not know it, and Dolly—this is
A word I have used more times in the year since we adopted her than

Ever before—*lunged*, she must have, though I only heard the cry,
And I ran, *I* lunged, pants half down, grotesque, I pried her jaw open,
I freed the cat. I am covered now in reminders, writing this, criss-
Crossing lines on a madman's map, my body looks like a tree someone

Has plied for water, slashed for sustenance. But I am dried out.
I give nothing. I can only kill you. For Della, there could be no progeny.
When I brought her to the vet, blood congealing and dripping in ribbons
From her mouth, I had to check the box. "Altered," or whatever it was.

Fixed, maybe. That's what we call it. She would have no pit cherries,
Whether or not they waited, in her womb, on the cob. So, what did she
Produce? By what measure should we measure Della's life?
In the time since we got her, our lives began, mine and Mary's, together,

Our love blossomed, and Della was there. Della slept with us in the bed
While the dog lowed in her crate, Della ran down the porch to the door
When we came home, Della was our fluff on the wind, and this is it:
The silk floss tree also produces flowers, pink, and only on its crown.

They touch the blue sky. Clouds on the ground, tangled in the grass,
Flowers in the sky. By what should we measure a life? You know
What. Nobody killed our cat. Everybody did. That is the terrible
Thing. "Forgive me," the woman said, looking at me.

Notes

The epigraph from James Foster ahead of "The Leavings" comes from the paper, "Stellar Performance: Mechanisms Underlying Milky Way Orientation in Dung Beetles," *Philosophical Transactions of the Royal Society B* 372, no. 1717 (April 5, 2017).

Acknowledgments

"One Year in New Hampshire" was published in the *Bennington Review*

About the Author

Levin is the author of *Slonim Woods 9* (Crown, 2021), described by *Nylon* as "extraordinary, biting, observant," a memoir that vividly recounts his experience as a survivor of a college cult and offers a profound exploration of manipulation, resilience, and recovery.

He produced the Hulu docuseries *Stolen Youth*, which unflinchingly depicted the tragic consequences of coercive control and the remarkable resilience of its survivors. His essays and poems have appeared in *Provincetown Arts*, *Psychology Today*, and numerous other publications, and he has spoken and taught widely on the power of poetry, memoir, mental health, trauma recovery, and the psychology of coercion for both national media—including *Radiolab*—and classrooms across the country.

Levin lives in Los Angeles.

Four Way Books is grateful to those individuals who participated in our Build a Book Program. They are:

Anonymous (10), Robert Abrams, Debra Allbery, Maggie Anderson, Kathy Aponick, Sally Ball, Jean Ball, Victor Basta, Adria Bernardi, Richard Blanchard, Laurel Blossom, adam b. bohannon, Lee Briccetti, Anthony Cappo, Anne Babson Carter, Cyrus Cassells, Jennifer Christman, Peter Coyote, Kwame Dawes, Michael Anna de Armas, Brian Komei Dempster, Patrick Donnelly, Lynn Emanuel, Joan Frank, Rigoberto González, Rachel Eliza Griffiths, Catherine Grossman, Naomi Guttman and Jonathan Mead, Beth Harrison, Jeffrey Harrison, KT Herr, Carlie Hoffman, Melissa Hotchkiss, Thomas and Autumn Howard, Parker Howe Foundation, Catherine Hoyser, Linda Susan Jackson, Elizabeth Jackson, Liz Janik, Marilyn Johnson, Deborah and Maria Jonas-Walsh, Elizabeth J. Kandall, Maeve Kinkead, Lindsay and John Landes, David Lee and Jamila Trindle, Rodney Terich Leonard, Howard Levy, Owen Lewis and Susan Ennis, Ralph and Mary Ann Lowen, Maja Lukic, Ricardo Alberto Maldonado, Donna Masini, Cleopatra Mathis, Lupe Mendez, Dale Neal, Mary Jane Nealon, Kathy Nelson, Marilyn Nelson, Nicole Nevadunsky, Kimberly Nunes, Rebecca and Daniel Okrent, Cathy McArthur Palermo, Marcia Pelletiere, Megan Pinto, Martha Rhodes, Paula Rhodes, Laurie Rosenblatt, Lyris Schonholz, Soraya Shalforoosh, Jennifer Skeele, Mary Slechta, Page Hill Starzinger, Sarah Stone, Yerra Sugarman, Marjorie and Lew Tesser, Reed Turchi, Maria Walsh, Martha Webster and Robert Fuentes, Calvin Wei, George Whalen Jr., Mark Wunderlich, Kathleen Zimmerman, and Carol Zoref.